D0883199

MEET
Tom Longboat

SCHOLASTIC CANADA
BIOGRAPHY

ELIZABETH
MACLEOD

ILLUSTRATED BY
MIKE DEAS

Scholastic Canada Ltd.
Toronto New York London Auckland Sydney
Mexico City New Delhi Hong Kong Buenos Aires

Tom Longboat raced to the finish line as the crowd cheered wildly.

One of the top runners in the world, Tom amazed and excited race fans. With a big smile on his face, Tom often found the energy to zip ahead at the end of his races. Other runners would be left behind, gasping for breath.

Tom liked winning and hearing the crowds cheer for him.
But most of all, Tom loved to run.

Tom was born in Ohsweken on the Six Nations Reserve near Brantford, Ontario, in 1886. His Onondaga name is Gagwé:geh — it means "everything."

Tom's family grew vegetables and raised farm animals. But Tom's dad died when Tom was just five years old. The family became very poor.

Tom had many chores to do, but he still made time for fun. He liked to chase after the cows. Sometimes Tom would run with his cousin. People got used to seeing the two boys racing all over the reserve.

Already Tom loved to run.

When Tom was twelve, he was taken from his home and sent to a school for Indigenous children. He and the other kids had to be residents there, so places like this were known as residential schools.

Tom hated it. He was forced to give up his family and friends. He wasn't allowed to speak the Onondaga language. The children were treated badly and even beaten.

In his second year at the residential school, Tom escaped and ran home. But he was found and dragged back.

A few weeks later, Tom ran away again. This time he went to the home of his uncle, who hid him. Tom was finished with school.

When Tom was almost eighteen, he entered his first race. In May 1905, he lined up with other runners in Caledonia, Ontario. Tom led all the other runners for most of the race, but he ended up coming in second. Tom didn't like that. He wanted to be first.

In 1906, Tom entered the famous Around the Bay Road Race in Hamilton, Ontario. He was racing against some of the best runners in the world. No one thought Tom would do very well. But he had learned from his first race and trained carefully.

Tom kept up with the other runners. In fact he sprinted past them at the end. Even though Tom took a wrong turn near the finish line, he won in record time.

Tom didn't train the same way other runners did. They ran long distances every day. But Tom would do a long run one day and the next he would play lacrosse or walk.

People put Tom down for the way he trained. They blamed his Indigenous background. But switching between hard workouts and easier ones is how runners train today. Tom knew better than anyone what the best way for him to train was.

The way Tom ran was different too. In those days, most runners took long, high strides with their hands up and still. By keeping his feet close to the ground and his hands low, Tom saved energy as he ran. Not every race ended with a win, but Tom was becoming known as a top racer.

One of the most famous long-distance races in the world is the Boston Marathon. On April 19, 1907, Tom was at the starting line with the other runners, ready to run it. Snow and sleet flew in their faces as cold winds blew.

About forty minutes into the race, Tom was one of the front-runners. Then he noticed a train barrelling down the track in the distance. It was going to block the race route. That would force Tom to stop, and he'd lose his lead.

Tom put on a burst of speed to beat the train.

13

The marathon was almost over. Tom and another runner from Canada named Charlie Petch were far ahead of everyone else. The exhausted racers headed toward the steep hills near the end of the race.

Charlie decided to take the hills slowly and save his energy. Not Tom! He attacked the hills, running faster than ever. That sprint put Tom far out in front, and he won the race.

Back in Toronto, where Tom was living, crowds had gathered around telegraph offices. They held their breath waiting for updates on their hero.

Everyone was so happy to receive the news that Tom had won.

When Tom returned a few days later, tens of thousands of people were waiting for him at the train station. Bands played and people cheered.

A huge crowd paraded him to Toronto City Hall for an official reception. Tom Longboat was famous — not only in Canada, but all over the world.

The Olympic Games were scheduled to take place around London, England, in 1908. Everyone expected Tom to easily win the marathon event. But Tom knew it would be a tough race.

London was in the middle of a July heat wave. The race was scheduled for the afternoon, not the cool of the morning. The air was hot and humid as the runners lined up to start at Windsor Castle.

17

When the Olympic marathon started, Tom was running well. But he was having trouble breathing because of the heat.

Other runners were falling down in the hot sun. They were so exhausted that they couldn't go on. Would that happen to Tom? He'd never given up in the middle of a race.

Tom was one of the front-runners when disaster struck. He collapsed on the road! His heart was racing and he was so tired he was shaking.

Unable to finish the race, Tom had to be carried off the course. His Olympic dream was over. Tom was so disappointed that he thought about giving up running.

But Tom loved running too much to stop. So in December 1908, Tom agreed to race Dorando Pietri, a top runner from Italy. Dorando had also collapsed during the Olympics. Fans wanted a rematch.

The two men had to run around the track at Madison Square Garden in New York until they had done the same distance as a marathon. Crowds yelled as the runners circled.

The pair had run 256 laps when Dorando suddenly collapsed. The crowd cheered as Tom finished the race and won.

Two months later, Tom faced off against England's top runner, Alfie Shrubb, at Madison Square Garden. Tom got off to a slow start. Alfie was ahead by eight laps before the race was half over.

Then Tom started to close the gap. Alfie had begun to tire. Tom caught up. When Tom passed Alfie, the English runner gave up.

Tom was now the World Professional Marathon Champion. But big changes were ahead.

In 1914 World War I broke out. This was a series of
battles that took place mainly in Europe. But countries
around the world, including Canada, were also involved.

Tom wanted to do his part. So he gave up his running
and all the fame and prize money, and he enlisted. At first,
Tom ran races to help entertain the soldiers.

Then Tom went to France to fight alongside other Canadian soldiers.

He was with the 107th Pioneer Battalion, a group of soldiers made up mostly of young Indigenous men.

Tom carried messages and orders between soldiers and their leaders, racing over the rough, muddy ground. He was shot at and wounded twice. Once, he was injured so badly that he was declared dead!

But the general couldn't keep up and ordered Tom to slow down. It was only then that the general realized who his famous guide was.

Tom was so glad when the war ended. He returned to Canada in 1919.

After the war, life was very different for Tom. Running was not as popular. It had been replaced by team sports, such as hockey and baseball. Tom was still fast, but he couldn't make money from racing anymore. He had to get a new job.

Eventually, he found work as a street cleaner and garbage collector in Toronto. Some people made fun of him for having a job like that because he had once been so famous.

Then in the late 1920s, the Great Depression hit countries around the world, including Canada. Many people lost their jobs. People couldn't buy food for their families. Many had nowhere to live.

But Tom always had work throughout this tough time. He took care of his family, and they lived in a nice house.

Tom retired in 1944 and moved back to the Six Nations Reserve. It was good to speak the Onondaga language again. Tom enjoyed seeing old friends and family and being more connected with his community.

Five years later Tom died. But this world-famous athlete has never been forgotten.

In 1951, the Tom Longboat Award was created. Every year it's given to top Indigenous athletes. Tom was made a member of Canada's Sports Hall of Fame in 1955.

In 2008, June 4 was named Tom Longboat Day in Ontario. A race in his honour is run on this day each year. Tom would have liked these awards and honours. But most of all, he just loved to run!

Tom Longboat's Life

July 4, 1886   Thomas Charles Longboat is born on the Six Nations Reserve near Brantford, Ontario. His Onondaga name is Gagwé:geh.

1899   Tom is forced to attend the Mohawk Institute Residential School, but later escapes.

May 22, 1905   Tom begins racing. He finishes second in a race in Caledonia, Ontario.

October 18, 1906   Tom wins the Around the Bay Road Race in Hamilton, Ontario.

April 19, 1907   Tom wins the Boston Marathon in the record time of 2 hours, 24 minutes and 24 seconds. He is the first Indigenous runner to win the race.

July 24, 1908   Tom and many other runners collapse during the Olympic marathon.

February 6, 1909   Tom wins the title of World Professional Marathon Champion.

February 17, 1916   Tom signs up to fight in World War I. He becomes a dispatch runner in France.

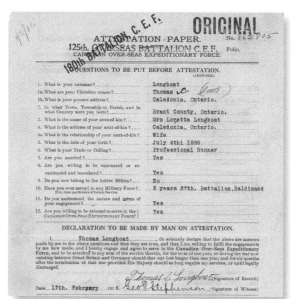

30   TOM LEADS IN A RACE WHILE HUGE CROWDS WATCH.

TOM'S SIGNED ENLISTMENT PAPERS. HIS BIRTHDAY IS RECORDED AS JULY 4, 1886.

1927	Tom begins working for Toronto's street cleaning department.
1944	Tom retires and moves back to the Six Nations Reserve.
January 9, 1949	Tom Longboat dies of pneumonia.
1951	The Tom Longboat Awards are set up to honour Indigenous athletes.
1955	Tom becomes a member of Canada's Sports Hall of Fame.
1972	The Woodland Cultural Centre, dedicated to the history and culture of the Iroquoian and Algonkian peoples, opens on the site of the residential school Tom attended.
2000	The Six Nations Reserve holds the first annual Tom Longboat Run.
2008	June 4 is named Tom Longboat Day in Ontario.
2015	A statue of Tom called *Challenge and Triumph* is unveiled. It was created by Mohawk artist David M. General.
2016	The Boston Marathon officially recognizes Indigenous runners for their contributions to long-distance running.

TOM BUYS A NEWSPAPER IN FRANCE.

THIS STATUE OF TOM NOW STANDS OUTSIDE THE YOUTH CENTRE ON THE SIX NATIONS RESERVE.

With lots of love for my great-nephew Theodore Thomas Rich.
Good luck with all the races you run throughout your life!
— E.M.
For Canada's future athletes
— M.D.

Many thanks to editor Erin O'Connor for getting this book across the finish line! Thanks also to the whole team at Scholastic, especially the book's illustrator, Mike Deas. I'm very grateful to Aisha Restoule General, who reviewed the book. Thanks also to my brothers, John and Douglas. Special thanks to Paul for being in it for the long run!
— E.M.

Scholastic is deeply grateful to Cindy Martin, who reviewed this book
on behalf of the Tom Longboat family.

Scholastic Canada Ltd.
604 King Street West, Toronto, Ontario M5V 1E1, Canada

Scholastic Inc.
557 Broadway, New York, NY 10012, USA

Scholastic Australia Pty Limited
PO Box 579, Gosford, NSW 2250, Australia

Scholastic New Zealand Limited
Private Bag 94407, Botany, Manukau 2163, New Zealand

Scholastic Children's Books
Euston House, 24 Eversholt Street, London NW1 1DB, UK

www.scholastic.ca

The illustrations were created using a blend of digital tools with traditional media. Sketches were created with a Wacom tablet and Photoshop, then traced onto watercolour paper, where colour and texture were added using gouache and watercolour paints. Ink was used to add the black line to finish the art.

Photos ©: cover and title page speech bubble, top right: fatmayilmaz/iStockphoto; Photos ©: 30 top right: Charles A. Aylett/Library and Archives Canada/C-014090; 30 bottom left: Canada's Sports Hall of Fame/Library and Archives Canada/PA-050294; 30 bottom right: (detail) attestation paper of Thomas Longboat, Library and Archives Canada, RG 150, accession 1992-93/166, box 5730-27, #862805, Thomas Longboat; 31 left: Canada. Dept. of National Defence/Library and Archives Canada/PA-001479; 31 right: Raymond Littlefield.

Library and Archives Canada Cataloguing in Publication

MacLeod, Elizabeth, author
    Meet Tom Longboat / Elizabeth MacLeod ; illustrated by Mike Deas.

(Scholastic Canada biography)
ISBN 978-1-4431-6391-0 (hardcover).--ISBN 978-1-4431-1397-7 (softcover)

    1. Longboat, Tom, 1887-1949--Juvenile literature. 2. Runners (Sports)--Canada--Biography--Juvenile literature. 3. Indian athletes--Canada--Biography--Juvenile literature. 4. Biographies-- I. Deas, Mike, 1982-, illustrator II. Title.

GV1061.15.L65M34 2019   j796.42'4092   C2018-903600-1

6 5 4 3 2 1   Printed in Malaysia 108   19 20 21 22 23